FOUR SEASONS
Math

Compiled by the Totline® Staff
strated by Marion Hopping Ekberg

D1301214

Totline® Books

Warren Publishing House
Everett, Washington

We wish to thank the following teachers, childcare workers, and parents for contributing some of the activities in this book: Betty Ruth Baker, Waco, TX; Ellen Bedford, Bridgeport, CT; Valerie Bielsker, Lenexa, KS; Janice Bodenstedt, Jackson, MI; Colraine Hunley, Doylestown, PA; Martha T. Lyon, Fort Wayne, IN; Kathy McCullough, St. Charles, IL; Susan M. Paprocki, Northbrook, IL; Susan Peters, Upland, CA; Beverly Qualheim, Marquette, MI; Bonnie Rogers, Olympia, WA; Debbie Rowley, Redmond, WA; Betty Silkunas, Lansdale, PA; Diane Thom, Maple Valley, WA; and Nancy C. Windes, Denver, CO.

Editor: Kathleen Cubley
Contributing Editors: Gayle Bittinger, Susan Hodges, Elizabeth McKinnon, Jean Warren
Copy Editor: Mae Rhodes
Proofreader: Kris Fulsaas
Editorial Assistant: Durby Peterson
Book Design and Layout: Sarah Ness
Cover Design and Production: Brenda Mann Harrison
Production Manager: Jo Anna Brock

ISBN: 1-57029-089-X

Library of Congress Catalog Card Number 96-60131
Printed in the United States of America
Published by: Warren Publishing House
                        P.O. Box 2250
                        Everett, WA 98203

20 19 18 17 16 15 14 13 12 11 10 9 8 7 6 5 4 3 2 1

Introduction

Numbers are fascinating to young children. One of the first questions they learn to respond to is, "How old are you?" Counting things in their environment—hands, fingers, blocks, friends—becomes second nature to them.

This book, *Four Seasons Math,* gives you many ideas for introducing numbers and simple math concepts to young children. With a chapter for each season of the year, you will find math activities that relate to what your children are interested in right now. Summer activities will find you counting ants at a picnic and flowers in a garden. Fall provides suggestions for harvest and leaf math games. Winter offers many holiday counting rhymes as well as snowy day math ideas. Spring brings more counting fun with activity suggestions for your children to explore bunnies and butterflies.

As with all Totline® Publications, the activity ideas in this book are developmentally appropriate and use only readily available materials. You and your children will enjoy the fun and easy-to-use ideas in *Four Seasons Math.*

Contents

Fall

Number Leaves

Cut five large leaves of different shapes out of posterboard. Cut each leaf into three sections. Label each section of the first leaf with the number 1, label each section of the second leaf with the number 2, and so on. In a large box, mix up all of the leaf pieces. Have your children put the leaves together by first matching the numbers and then putting the pieces together to form the leaf shapes.

Leaf Matching

Find five large leaves in good condition. Trace around each leaf on a separate piece of paper. Set out the leaves and the papers. Help your children count first the leaves and then the tracings. Show them how each real leaf has an identical tracing of it on one of the papers. Let the children take turns trying to match the real leaves to the leaf tracings.

How Many Leaves?

Place five to ten leaves in a see-through container such as a glass bowl. Ask your children to guess how many leaves are in the container. Take out the leaves and count them together. Try again with a different number of leaves.

Felt Leaf Game

Cut a bare tree shape out of brown felt and place it on a flannelboard. Cut out 10 to 20 small leaf shapes. Ask one of your children to place a particular number of leaves on the tree. With the group, count the number of leaves as you remove them. Ask the next child to place a different number of leaves on the tree. Continue until each child has had a turn.

Counting Apples

Place five to ten apples in front of your children. Have them count the apples. Ask them to close their eyes while you remove some of the apples. Help the children figure out how many apples are gone. Repeat as long as interest lasts.

Apple Game

Glue a felt tree shape onto each of five cardboard squares. Number the squares from 1 to 5. Cut 15 apple shapes out of felt. To play the game, have one of your children identify the number on one of the squares and place that number of apples on the tree.

Nut Collections

For each child, print a number on the outside of a paper sack. In each sack, place one or two *more* nuts or one or two *fewer* nuts than the number written on the outside of the sack. Give your children the sacks and set out a bowl of extra nuts. Let the children take out the nuts and count them. Have the children place the correct number of nuts back in their sacks by taking one or two nuts from the bowl or placing one or two extra nuts in the bowl.

Mixed Nuts

Set out a bowl containing a variety of unshelled nuts. Let your children count and sort the nuts. If a scale is available, encourage the children to weigh the nuts.

Extension: When your children have finished counting the nuts, shell the nuts and have a taste test. (Be aware that nuts should not be served to children under the age of 3.)

Pulling Up Carrots

Purchase ten carrots with green, leafy tops. "Plant" the carrots in a big tub of dirt so that they look as if they are actually growing. Ask one of your children to pull up three carrots, a second child to pull up one carrot, and so on, until the tub is empty. Then replant the carrots and start the game again.

Veggie Sort and Count

Set out several sizes and colors of one kind of vegetable. For example, if you are using potatoes, set out small, medium, and large potatoes with red, yellow, and dark brown skins. Let your children sort the potatoes into piles by color or by size. Then have them count how many potatoes there are in each pile. If desired, have them arrange the potatoes from smallest to largest.

Shopping Game

Save picture labels from cans or packages of familiar vegetables (tomatoes, corn, beans, peas, carrots, etc.). To make the game, prepare a shopping list for your children. On a sheet of heavy paper, glue a tomato label, corn label, and bean label. In front of the tomato label, write the number 4; in front of the corn label, write the number 2; and in front of the bean label, write the number 3. Trim the remaining labels and glue them on separate index cards. Arrange ten vegetable cards on a table, including four tomato labels, two corn labels, and three bean labels. Give one of the children the shopping list. Let him or her "shop" for the vegetables by selecting the appropriate number of tomato, corn, and bean labels from the table. Make additional shopping lists according the kinds of labels you collected.

Graphing Veggies

Hang a piece of butcher paper on a wall directly above the floor or a table. Draw a picture of a carrot, a potato, and a tomato at the top of the paper. Set out several blocks that are identical in size and color. Ask your children to name which of the pictured vegetables they like best. Have each child place a block under the picture of the vegetable he or she likes best. After each child has had a turn, ask the children to count the number of blocks under each picture. How many children like carrots? Potatoes? Tomatoes?

Variation: Instead of using blocks, have each child place a sticker on the paper under the picture of his or her favorite vegetable.

Counting Spider Prints

Using a black ink pad, let your children make fingerprints on small index cards. Help them turn their fingerprints into spiders by drawing eight legs on each one with a fine point marker. Have each child count the number of spiders he or she has created. Write the corresponding number at the bottom of each child's card.

Spider Stamping

Use the illustration at left as a guide for drawing a spider web. Draw the web with a black felt tip marker on a piece of white paper. Photocopy the spider web for each of your children. Write a number from 1 to 5 on each paper web. Hand out the papers and set out a washable black ink pad. Have your children identify the number on their paper and make the corresponding number of fingerprint "spiders" on their web. (Follow the directions in the above activity to make fingerprint spiders.)

Big Black Spiders

Let your children help paint both sides of eight paper plates black. When the paint has dried, attach a large white sticker to each plate. Number the stickers from 1 to 8. Cut black crepe paper into long strips. Have the children choose a plate and identify the number on it. Then let them attach that many crepe-paper strips to the plate to create a spider with legs. Attach strings to the completed spiders and hang them from the ceiling to use for future counting activities.

Boots for the Spider

Cut a spider shape out of black felt (make sure to cut eight legs). Then cut eight boot shapes out of a contrasting color of felt. Place the spider shape on a flannelboard. When you reach line five in the poem below, let one of your children place the boots on the spider's legs. Take turns until each child has a chance to place the boots on the spider's legs.

How many boots should a spider buy

To keep his feet nice and dry?

Let's count his feet and then we'll know.

I can count—watch me go!

One, two, three, four, five, six, seven, eight.

Eight new boots is what he should buy—

That will keep the spider dry.

Janice Bodenstedt

Pumpkin Matching Cards

Divide ten index cards into pairs. On the first pair, draw one pumpkin on each card. On the second pair, draw two pumpkins on each card. On the third pair, draw three pumpkins on each card, and so on for the remaining pairs. Mix up the cards and give them to your children. Let them take turns finding the cards with the matching number of pumpkins and placing them side by side.

Variation: Mix up all of the cards and arrange them face-down on a table. Let your children take turns playing concentration with the cards.

Pumpkin Counting

Cut several pumpkin shapes out of felt. Place the shapes on a flannelboard. Let your children manipulate the shapes as you recite simple counting rhymes like the one below.

Here is a pumpkin,

And here is a pumpkin,

And another pumpkin, I see.

Shall we count them?

Are you ready?

One, two, three!

Traditional

Extension: As your children become more proficient in counting, encourage them to sing and count as follows:

Sung to: "The Paw-Paw Patch"

One little, two little, three little pumpkins.

Four little, five little, six little pumpkins.

Seven little, eight little, nine little pumpkins.

Ten little pumpkins in the pumpkin patch.

Adapted Traditional

Pumpkin Teeth Game

Cut five pumpkin shapes out of orange felt. On each pumpkin, draw a simple jack-o'-lantern face with a large smile, but no teeth. Number the pumpkins from 1 to 5. Cut 15 tooth shapes out of black felt. Place the pumpkins on a flannelboard. Have your children take turns identifying the number on each pumpkin and placing the appropriate number of teeth in its mouth.

Ghost Matching

Use a black felt tip marker to draw ten identical ghost shapes on index cards. On each ghost, draw a different number of dots, starting with one dot and ending with ten dots. Cut the ghosts out. Lay the ghosts on a large piece of white paper and trace around each one with a black felt tip marker. Remove the ghost shapes and number the outlines from 1 to 10, in random order. Add a few details, such as a pumpkin patch, a fence, and a cat, to the page to make a "spooky" Halloween scene. Set out the picture and the ghost shapes. Let your children take turns matching the ghost shapes to their tracings on the scene.

Turkey Feathers

Cut 5 turkey body shapes from brown felt and 15 tail feather shapes from red, yellow, and orange felt. Number the turkey body shapes from 1 to 5 and place them on a flannelboard. Put the feather shapes in a pile. To play the game, have your children take turns selecting a turkey, identifying the number written on it, and adding that many tail feathers to it.

Estimating Kernels

Place some popcorn kernels in a small clear-plastic container and let your children estimate how many kernels it contains. After everyone has had a turn estimating, pour out the kernels and count them together.

Nut Pie Game

Attach five foil tart pans to squares of heavy paper. Number the squares from 1 to 5. Fill the tart pans with playdough to make "pies." Provide your children with a basket containing 15 unshelled nuts. Let the children take turns decorating the pies by placing the appropriate number of nuts on top of each one.

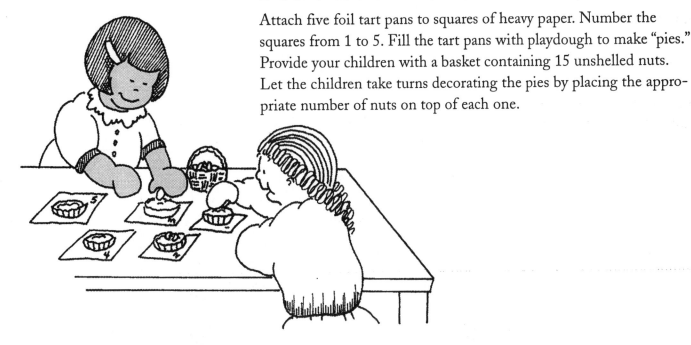

Pie Puzzles

Cut three identical circles (about 12 inches in diameter) out of posterboard. Using felt tip markers, decorate each circle in a different color to make three kinds of "pie." Cut one pie in half, one into fourths, and one into eighths. Mix up the pieces and let your children have fun putting them together in various ways to create three whole pies.

Variation: For younger children, set out the pieces for one pie at a time.

Snowball Counting

Use large index cards to make a set of five counting cards. Draw one dot on the first card, two dots on the second card, and so on. Lay the cards on a table and set out 15 cotton ball "snowballs." Let your children count the snowballs as they place them on the dots on the cards.

Snowball Hunt

Hide cotton balls around the room. Give each of your children an empty egg carton with the cups labeled from 1 to 12. Let the children walk around the room looking for the hidden "snowballs." Encourage them to put their snowballs into the cups in numerical order. Once all the snowballs have been found, count them together.

Boot Mix-Up

Cut several identical snow boot shapes out of various colors of construction paper. Divide the boot shapes into pairs. Use a felt tip marker to draw a different design on each pair of boots. Cover the boots with clear self-stick paper, if desired. Place the boots on the floor and mix them up. Let your children find the matching pairs of boots.

Variation: Instead of using boot shapes, cut out other winter clothing shapes such as scarves, hats, or coats.

Mitten Matching

From wallpaper or gift-wrap scraps, cut out ten pairs of mittens. Use a felt tip marker to number one mitten with the number 1, another with the number 2, and so on up to 10. Mark the other ten mittens with corresponding numbers of dots. Let your children match each numbered mitten to the mitten with the appropriate number of dots.

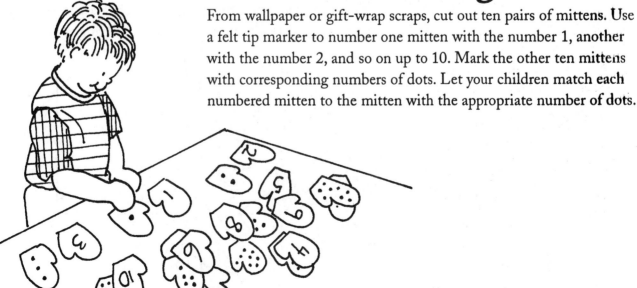

Plant-a-Forest Game

Paint a shoebox brown and cut six slots in the lid of the box. Number the slots from 1 to 6. Cut six tree shapes out of green construction paper and attach them to craft sticks. Number the trees from 1 to 6. To play the game, have your children identify the numbers on the trees and insert them into the matching numbered slots in the shoebox lid.

Christmas Shapes

Cut a large triangular tree from green felt, a square tree trunk from brown felt, circular tree decorations from red felt, and square and rectangular presents from any colors of felt you like. Place the shapes on a flannelboard to create a Christmas scene. Ask your children, one at a time, to find a square, a circle, a rectangle, etc., in the scene. After everyone has had a turn finding a shape, change the game by pointing to an object on the flannelboard and letting your children call out its shape.

Triangle Tree Puzzle

From green felt, cut out nine triangles. Arrange them on a large piece of felt to make a triangular tree shape. Outline the finished tree shape with a felt tip marker or fabric paint. Encourage your children to fit all nine triangles into the large tree shape. Help your children think of ways to turn the triangles to get them to fit.

Variation: For younger children, you may wish to use a felt tip marker or fabric paint to outline the nine smaller triangles within the tree shape, showing their placement.

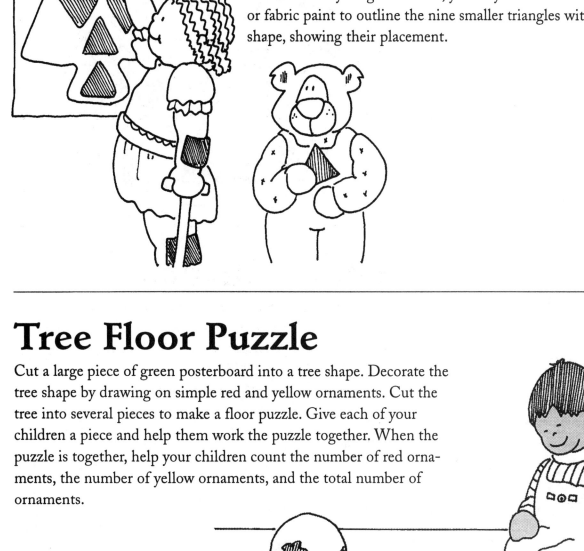

Tree Floor Puzzle

Cut a large piece of green posterboard into a tree shape. Decorate the tree shape by drawing on simple red and yellow ornaments. Cut the tree into several pieces to make a floor puzzle. Give each of your children a piece and help them work the puzzle together. When the puzzle is together, help your children count the number of red ornaments, the number of yellow ornaments, and the total number of ornaments.

Counting Pine Cones

Set out a box of pine cones. Ask your children to count out three pine cones, five pine cones, etc. Then have them each select a pine cone and pull the scales off of it. Ask them to count the scales. Have them compare numbers. Which pine cone had the most scales? Which had the fewest?

Pine Cone Game

Cut five evergreen tree shapes out of green felt and five pine cone shapes out of brown felt. Number the tree shapes from 1 to 5. Number the pine cone shapes with dots from 1 to 5. Place the tree shapes on a flannelboard. Have your children take turns selecting a pine cone, counting the dots on it, and placing it on the appropriate tree.

Star of David Game

To make ten stars, cut twenty 4-inch triangles out of posterboard. Make each six-pointed star by placing one triangle point-up and gluing another triangle point-down on top of it. Use a felt tip marker to number five of the stars from 1 to 5. Then draw corresponding numbers of dots on the other five stars. Mix up the stars and let your children take turns finding the matching pairs.

Hanukkah Candles

Cut a menorah shape, nine candle shapes, and nine flame shapes out of felt. Place the menorah on a flannelboard and arrange the nine candles to stand in the menorah. Place one of the flame shapes on top of the middle candle. Explain that in a real menorah, the candle in the center (the *shammash*) would be used to light the other candles. Then let your children take turns placing flame shapes on the eight remaining candles as you read the poem below. Remove all the flames after each verse so that the next child can "light" the appropriate number of candles.

Eight little candles in a row,

Waiting to join the holiday glow.

The first night we light candle number one.

Hanukkah time has now begun.

The second night we light candles one and two.

Hanukkah's here—there's lots to do.

The third night we light all up to three.

Hanukkah's here—there's lots to see.

The fourth night we light all up to four,

Each now a part of the Hanukkah lore.

The fifth night we light all up to five,

Helping our Hanukkah come alive.

The sixth night we light all up to six.

Hanukkah's here—special food to fix.

The seventh night we light all up to seven.

The glow of each candle reaches to Heaven.

The eighth night we light all up to eight.

Hanukkah's here—let's celebrate!

Jean Warren

Arranging Stars

Cut out several sizes of stars. Let your children arrange them in order from smallest to largest or from largest to smallest. Then have your children count the stars.

Star Folders

Draw eight stars on the inside of a file folder and number them from 1 to 8. Draw matching star shapes on construction paper or index cards and cut them out. Use dots to number the star cutouts from 1 to 8. Give your children the file folder and the cutout stars. Let them take turns matching the numbers by placing the cutouts on the corresponding outlines on the file folder.

Teddy Bear Measuring

Collect a variety of teddy bears and place them in a pile on the floor. Let your children work in groups or take turns lining the bears up from largest to smallest and from smallest to largest. Have the children weigh the teddy bears on a scale. Which one is the heaviest? Which one is the lightest? Encourage the children to find different ways to measure the teddies, such as measuring tails or ears.

Hint: If you wish to have your children bring in their own teddy bears for this activity, be sure to let parents know in advance. Bring in your teddy bear, too!

Teddy Bear Math

Use the teddy bears from the Teddy Bear Measuring activity on this page to let your children try the math activities that follow.

- Ask your children to sort the teddy bears by categories such as color, size, or those with bows and those without. Have them count the number of bears in each category.

- Have your children form different sets of teddy bears, such as **five** brown bears, three white bears, or two large bears.

Mailbox Game

Cut 20 heart shapes out of red construction paper. Use a hole punch to punch from one to five holes in each heart. Then cut a slot in each of five shoeboxes to make mailboxes. (If desired, paint the boxes blue, or cover them with blue self-stick paper.) Number the boxes from 1 to 5. To play the game, let one of your children select one of the hearts, count the number of holes in it, and mail it in the corresponding mailbox.

Heart Number Necklaces

For each of your children, cut several heart shapes out of red, pink, and white construction paper. Punch a hole in each heart shape. Hide the hearts around your room and let the children hunt for them. (Make sure everyone finds some.) When the heart hunt is over, have each child bring you his or her heart collection. Together, count the hearts and write that number on one of them. Let the child string the hearts on a piece of red yarn to make a necklace.

How Many Hearts?

Place several candy hearts in a baby food jar. Let each of your children guess how many candies are in the jar. When everyone has guessed, empty the jar and count the candies together.

Variation: Instead of candy hearts, use heart-shaped erasers or buttons.

Match the Hearts

From an old deck of playing cards, remove the numbered cards in the heart suit. Cut each card in half crosswise so that a number shows on both halves. Let your children take turns matching the corresponding numbers.

Counting the Days

Waiting for holidays can be very difficult for young children. To make the waiting a little easier, try one or more of the following activities.

Countdown Calendar

On butcher paper, make a large, simple calendar with one square for each of the days remaining before the holiday and one for the actual holiday. Write the dates in the squares. Decorate the holiday square. In each of the other squares, write down a simple end-of-the-day activity such as singing a song. At the end of each day, do the activity with your children and let one of them cross off that day. As a group, count the days remaining before the holiday.

Sticker Days

Count the number of days left before the holiday. On a sheet of construction paper, write a number for each of those days, starting with the highest number and counting backward. For example, if there are five days left, your paper would read "5 4 3 2 1." Decorate the paper with holiday symbols, if you wish. Show the paper to your children. Each day, give one of your children a sticker to put on the highest number. Help the children count the remaining numbers to find out how many days are left before the holiday.

Hint: You may wish to start this activity when the days remaining before a holiday are equal to the number of children in your group. That way each child will have a chance to put a sticker on a number.

Chain Calendars

Collect several sheets of construction paper in colors appropriate to the holiday you are counting down toward. For each of your children, cut one strip of construction paper for each of the days remaining before the holiday. Give the strips to your children. Help them tape or staple their strips together to make links in a chain. Attach each chain to a holiday shape cut out of additional construction paper. Hang the calendars on a wall at your children's eye level. Each day, let the children remove one of the links from their chain and count the remaining days.

Hint: These individual calendars are great for children whose families celebrate different holidays. For example, you could have calendars for Hanukkah, Christmas, and Kwanzaa.

Spring

St. Patrick's Day Graph

A few days before St. Patrick's Day, send parents a reminder to let their children wear green on that day. On St. Patrick's Day, make a clothing graph like the one shown in the illustration. Let your children place stickers in the spaces next to the types of green clothing they are wearing. Then help the children count the stickers in each row. Which type of clothing has the most stickers in its row? Which has the fewest?

Shamrock Books

For each child, number five pieces of construction paper from 1 to 5 and staple them together on the left-hand side to make a book. Give each of your children one of the books and 15 shamrock stickers. Have the children place the appropriate number of stickers on each page. Let the children "read" their books to you by counting the number of stickers on each page.

Stamping Shamrocks

On each of several sheets of paper, write the numerals 1 to 10 in a row. Give each child one of the numbered sheets, a shamrock rubber stamp, and an ink pad. Sing the song below and have the children stamp on top of each number at the appropriate time.

Sung to: "The Paw-Paw Patch"

One little, two little,

Three little shamrocks.

Four little, five little,

Six little shamrocks.

Seven little, eight little,

Nine little shamrocks.

Ten green shamrocks

All across my page.

Kathy McCullough

St. Patrick's Day Lotto

To make gameboards, cut posterboard into 9-inch squares. With a marker, divide each gameboard into nine squares and place a different St. Patrick's Day sticker in each square. For each gameboard, make a set of nine matching game cards on 3-inch squares cut from posterboard. Tape a resealable plastic bag to the back of each of gameboard to make a holder for the game cards. Then let your children play matching games by placing the game cards on top of the corresponding squares on the gameboards.

Weighing Gold

Collect rocks in a variety of sizes and shapes. In an area away from your children, spray-paint the rocks gold. Allow the rocks to dry completely. Set out the pieces of "gold" and a scale. Let the children take turns weighing the gold. Help them read the numbers on the scale as needed. After the children have finished weighing the gold, let them sort the gold into piles by size. How many are in each pile?

Leprechaun's Gold

Make a "pot of gold" by covering a coffee can with black construction paper and filling it with "coins" cut from yellow paper. Choose one of your children to be the Leprechaun and give him or her the pot of gold. Let one child begin by saying, "Leprechaun, will you give me some gold?" Have the Leprechaun reply, "Yes, I will, when a number I'm told." Have the child roll a die and name the number that comes up on it. Then have the Leprechaun give the child that number of gold pieces. Continue the game until everyone has had a turn, and then choose another child to be the Leprechaun.

Leprechaun Game

Cut ten simple leprechaun shapes, such as those shown in the illustration, out of green construction paper. Cover the shapes with clear self-stick paper for durability. Use a permanent marker to write a number on each of the shapes. Then give each of your children a leprechaun shape and a small bag of gold-painted pebbles. Let your children place the appropriate number of pebbles on their leprechaun shapes. Have your children trade shapes with one another and continue the game.

Variation: Instead of using gold-painted pebbles for the counters, laminate (or cover with clear self-stick paper) a sheet of gold wrapping paper and cut out lots of half-inch circles. You could also use this method of "gold making" for the Leprechaun's Gold activity on page 38.

Number Line

Tape together strips of posterboard to make a long number line and place it on the floor. Mark off ten sections and number them. Collect several different small objects relating to St. Patrick's Day, such as a paper shamrock, a pot of pretend gold, a leprechaun's hat, and something green. Place each object in one of the numbered sections. Have your children look at the number line while you ask them questions such as these: "What number is the shamrock on? What object is on number 7? Where is the leprechaun's hat?"

Bunny Predictions

Let your children bring in stuffed bunnies from home (or collect a variety of bunnies yourself). Gather the children into a circle. Let each child show his or her bunny to the rest of the children and then place it on the floor in the center of the circle. Ask them to show their bunnies and to guess which bunny is the shortest, which is the tallest, and which bunnies have the longest and shortest ears. Let them use yarn to measure the bunnies' heights and ears. Compare the children's guesses with the actual answers.

Hopping Bunnies

Let your children pretend to be hopping bunnies. Then let one child be the leader and say, "Hopping bunnies jump _____ times," filling in the blank with a number from 1 to 10. Have the rest of the children hop that number of times. Let each child have a turn at being the leader.

Bunny Categorizing

Cut out several pictures of bunnies. Let your children categorize the bunny pictures by color. Have the children count the bunnies in each group. Then mix up the pictures and have the children sort them into other categories, such as size or kind of ears. Help the children count the bunnies in each category.

Bunnies on the Hill

Cut ten simple bunny shapes, such as those in the illustration, out of felt. Use a permanent felt tip marker to number the bunnies from 1 to 10. Cut a green hill out of felt and use it for a background on a flannelboard. Have your children pick a number between 1 and 10. Then let them find the corresponding bunny and place it on the hill. Let the children take turns until all of the bunnies are on the hill.

Number Eggs

Find ten plastic eggs of the same color. Using a permanent felt tip marker, number the top of each plastic egg with a numeral from 1 to 10. Mark the bottoms of the eggs with corresponding numbers of dots. Place the tops and bottoms of the eggs in a basket. Let your children match the numbers to the dots.

Extension: After your children have correctly matched the egg halves, set out a dish of dry beans. Let the children fill each egg with the appropriate number of beans.

Pass the Basket Game

You will need a basket and enough plastic eggs for each of your children to have at least one. Have the children sit in a circle. Show them the basket and have them guess how many eggs will fit in it. Then put an egg in and say, "One." Explain that you will pass the basket around the circle. As a child gets the basket, he or she should put one egg in and then say how many eggs are in the basket. Continue passing the basket around the circle until it is full. Count the eggs with your children.

Egg Poll

Draw a line down the center of a sheet of chart paper to make two columns. At the top of one column, glue a picture of a fried egg. At the top of the other column, glue a picture of scrambled eggs. Write the names of your children on pieces of paper or plain address labels. Ask each child if he or she prefers eating fried eggs or scrambled eggs. Then let the child tape his or her name on the chart in the appropriate column. When everyone's name is on the chart, count the choices in each column together to discover your group's preference.

Counting Game

Collect ten plastic eggs. Across the open end of one half of each egg, glue a cardboard circle. Write the numbers 1 through 10 on smaller yellow paper circles and glue them to the cardboard circles to make "yolks." Have each of your children open an egg and name the number inside it. Then have the children take turns placing the eggs in numerical order.

Variation: Make fried egg shapes out of index cards and yellow construction paper. Number the yolks from 1 to 10. Then place one shape inside each plastic egg.

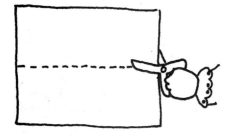

Open the Barn Doors

Cut several sheets of construction paper in half lengthwise. Fold the ends of each cut piece into the middle so that the ends touch. Draw a simple outline of a barn door on the front of each flap. Write a number on one of the doors and draw a corresponding number of dots on the other door. Continue until you have a paper barn for each of your children. Set out the paper barns, rubber stamps of farm animals, and ink pads. Let each child select a numbered barn. Have them identify the number on their barn door and stamp that many animals inside the barn.

Animal Math

Cut several farm animal pictures out of magazines. Reinforce them with clear self-stick paper for durability, if you wish. Arrange a piece of yarn in a circle on a table or the floor to represent a fenced area. Place the animal pictures inside and outside the fence as needed while you tell a simple story that involves counting. For example, you might begin the story like this: "Two cows were standing in a field inside a fence. A pig came and stood beside them. How many animals are inside the fence now? The two cows left to find better grass to eat. Now how many animals are inside the fence?"

Butterfly Matchups

Collect six cardboard toilet tissue tubes to use for butterfly bodies. Cut 3-inch slots opposite each other on one end of each tube. Make six pairs of butterfly wings by cutting three paper plates into four sections each. Draw matching sets of dots on each pair of wings. Let your children take turns putting the butterflies together by finding the matching pairs of wings and inserting them into the slots in the cardboard tube bodies.

Butterfly Puzzles

Cut five large butterfly shapes out of construction paper. Number one wing of each butterfly with a numeral from 1 to 5. Number the other wing of each butterfly with dots from 1 to 5. Cover the butterflies with clear self-stick paper and cut them in half down the center to make two puzzle pieces. Mix up the pieces and let one or two of your children at a time take turns finding the pieces and putting them together to make whole butterflies.

Raindrops on Umbrellas

Draw five large umbrella shapes on a piece of butcher paper. Write a numeral from 1 to 5 on each umbrella, and then attach that number of self-stick Velcro dots to the edge of each umbrella. Cover a piece of light blue construction paper with clear self-stick paper, and then cut out 15 raindrops. Attach the other half of the Velcro dots to the backs of the raindrops. Let your children take turns attaching the appropriate number of raindrops to the umbrellas.

Five Umbrellas

Cut one umbrella shape out of each of the following colors of felt: red, blue, green, yellow, and purple. Place the shapes on a flannelboard. As you read each verse of the following poem, remove the appropriate umbrella.

Five umbrellas stood by the back door.

The red one went outside, then there were four.

Four umbrellas pretty as can be.

The blue one went outside, then there were three.

Three umbrellas with nothing to do.

The green one went outside, then there were two.

Two umbrellas not having much fun.

The yellow one went outside, then there was one.

Just one umbrella alone in the hall.

The purple one went outside, and that was all.

Jean Warren

Rainbow Counting

From posterboard, cut five rainbow shapes. Use a black felt tip marker to divide each shape lengthwise into five arches. Color the top arch on each shape red, the next arch orange, the next yellow, the next green, and the last arch blue. Then number the top arch on each shape with the number 1, the second with 2, the third with 3, and so on, down to 5. Cut each rainbow apart into 5 arches. Mix up the arches and let your children make rainbows by assembling the arches in numerical sequence.

Rain Watching

Make a rain gauge by using a permanent marker to mark ½-inch increments on the side of a clear-plastic jar (such as a peanut butter jar with the label removed). Place the jar outside. Each day, have one of your children bring the jar inside to check for rainfall accumulation. Keep track of the rainfall on a chart.

Summer

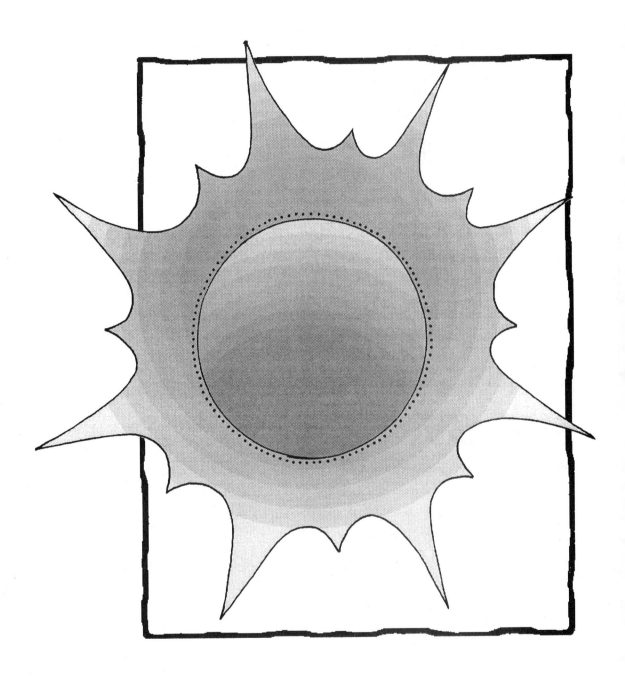

Sunshine Poll

Discuss with your children how the sun makes it hot outside during the summer months. After your discussion, make a chart to show how your children feel about sunny, hot days. Draw two columns on a large sheet of butcher paper. Draw a sun with a happy face at the top of one column, and label the column "I like it when it's hot." At the top of the other column, draw a sun with a sad face, and print "I don't like it when it's hot." Ask each child if he or she likes it when it's hot, and then put a check mark in the corresponding column. When all of your children have voted, have them help you count the votes. What do your children think about hot days?

Sun Rays

From yellow posterboard, cut out five circle "suns." Number the suns from 1 to 5. Give the suns and 20 spring-type clothespins to one of your children. Let the child clip the appropriate number of clothespin "rays" to each of the suns.

Variation: Place the numbered suns on a piece of construction paper. Glue the matching number of yellow yarn "rays" to the paper around each of the suns. Remove the suns and give them and the sheet of paper to one of your children. Let him or her match the suns to the corresponding number of rays.

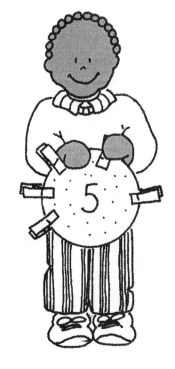

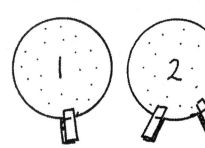

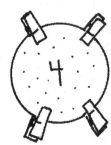

Number Cones

Cut five cone shapes out of brown felt. Number the cones from 1 to 5 using dots. Cut five ice cream scoop shapes out of white or pink felt. Number the scoops from 1 to 5 using numbers. Place the cones on a flannelboard. Let your children take turns counting the dots on the cones and placing scoops with the corresponding numbers on them.

Matching Cones

Draw an ice cream cone shape on each of eight index cards. Make matching cards by drawing one ice cream scoop on two cones, two ice cream scoops on two more cones, and so on. Cover the index cards with clear self-stick paper for durability, if desired. Mix up the cards and let your children take turns finding the cones with the matching number of ice cream scoops.

Variation: Mix up the cards and place them face down on a table. Let your children take turns playing ice cream concentration.

Buried Treasure

Fill a shallow box with sand and hide five small shells in it. Let your children search for the "buried treasure," one or two at a time. When they have found as many of the shells as they can, ask them to count the shells. Provide a sifter for the children to use when searching for the treasure, if desired.

Shell Pattern Fun

Cut shell shapes out of felt. Arrange some of the felt shell shapes in a pattern on a flannelboard. Show your children how to use more shell shapes to make the same pattern underneath the first pattern. Then make a new pattern with the shell shapes and let your children work together to create the same pattern underneath it.

Variation: As your children become more skilled in repeating patterns, make a shell pattern on the flannelboard and ask them to extend it.

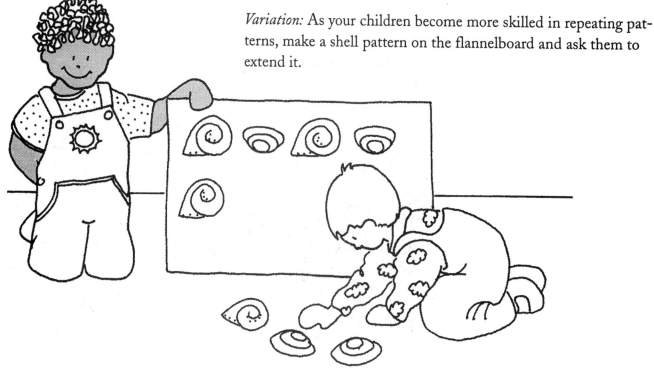

Shell Scenes

Draw simple beach scenes showing brown sand and blue water and sky on five sheets of construction paper. Number the papers from 1 to 5. Set out the beach scenes and 15 real shells. (You can purchase shells at craft stores.) Have your children take turns identifying the number on one of the papers and placing the corresponding number of shells on that beach scene. Repeat for the remaining papers.

Shell Counting

Place 15 to 20 shells in a sand bucket. Gather your children into a circle. Pass the bucket around the circle and ask your children to guess how many shells are in the bucket. After everyone has guessed, dump out the bucket and count the shells together. If interest lasts, change the number of shells in the bucket and play the game again.

Sunflower Math

Bring in a sunflower to show your children. Ask them to guess how many petals are on the sunflower. Together, count the petals. Next, draw a sunflower face on each of ten index cards. Make matching cards by adding one petal to two of the sunflower faces, two petals to two more faces, three petals to two more, and so on, until you have made five pairs of cards. Let your children take turns mixing up the cards and finding the matching pairs.

Magnetic Flower Power

Attach pieces of magnetic tape to a large collection of paper flower cutouts. Place one magnetic plastic number on a magnetic surface, such as a magnetboard, refrigerator, metal door, or nonaluminum baking sheet, and let your children take turns placing that number of flowers next it. Repeat with other numbers.

Variation: For an independent activity, place one or two number magnets on the magnetic surface and set the flower cutouts nearby. Then, as your children notice the magnets, they can place the flowers next to them.

Flower Number Book

Cut out six blue felt squares, all the same size. Cut six flower pot shapes out of brown felt. Glue a flower pot shape to each of the squares and stack them on top of each other, front sides up. Sew the squares together by stitching a seam down the left side. Use a permanent felt tip marker to number the flower pot shapes from 1 to 6. Cut out flower stem shapes from green felt. Glue one stem to pot number 1, two stems to pot number 2, and so on, up to number 6. Cut out leaves and add them to the stems, if desired. Sew a button onto the felt at the top of each stem. Cut 20 flower shapes out of various colors of felt. Cut a small slit in the center of each flower shape. Give the book and the flower shapes to one of your children. Let the child look through the book and button the corresponding number of flowers to each page.

Flower Matching Game

Cut 15 flower shapes out of construction paper. Glue each flower shape to the top of a craft stick. Place a small amount of playdough in the bottom of each of five paper cups. In each cup, "plant" a different number of flowers (from 1 to 5). Number five index cards from 1 to 5. Set out the cups and the cards. Let your children take turns selecting a cup, counting the flowers in it, and finding the card with that number.

Counting Flowers

For each of your children, write a number at the top of a sheet of construction paper and draw that number of flower stems on the paper. Count the total number of flower stems you have drawn and cut an equal number of simple flower shapes out of various colors of construction paper (or purchase ready-made paper flower shapes from a school supply store). Place the flower shapes in a pile. Give the flower stem papers to the children. Have each child identify the number on his or her paper and count out that number of flowers from the pile. Then let the children glue their flowers at the tops of the stems on their papers.

Flower Children

Measure each of your children and cut a flower stem of the same height out of butcher paper. Let your children compare their stems to their heights. Can they find anything else in the room that is the same length? Attach the flower stems to a bulletin board. Let your children decorate large flower shapes to attach to the top of their stems.

Dandelion Hunt

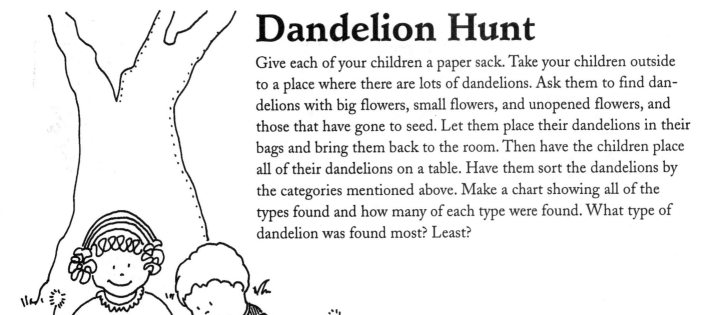

Give each of your children a paper sack. Take your children outside to a place where there are lots of dandelions. Ask them to find dandelions with big flowers, small flowers, and unopened flowers, and those that have gone to seed. Let them place their dandelions in their bags and bring them back to the room. Then have the children place all of their dandelions on a table. Have them sort the dandelions by the categories mentioned above. Make a chart showing all of the types found and how many of each type were found. What type of dandelion was found most? Least?

Daisy Bunnies

Hold up a daisy for your children to see. Show them how to carefully pick off the petals, counting them as you go, until there are just two petals left at the top. Now when you hold up the daisy, it looks like a bunny. Help the children find daisies for making their own bunnies. Remind them to leave two petals at the top.

Flag Matchups

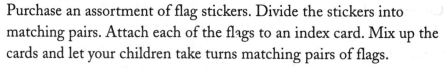

Purchase an assortment of flag stickers. Divide the stickers into matching pairs. Attach each of the flags to an index card. Mix up the cards and let your children take turns matching pairs of flags.

Variation: Mix up the cards and place them face down on a table. Let your children take turns playing flag concentration.

Stars and Stripes

Cut star shapes and stripes out of red, white, and blue felt. Place the stars and stripes in front of a flannelboard. Begin by playing a simple matching game. Put one of the stars on the flannelboard. Have one of your children place a matching-colored star below it. Then place a star and a stripe on the flannelboard. Ask another child to place matching shapes below those. Continue placing more stars and stripes on the flannelboard, making patterns with them as you do so. Help the children discover the patterns as they put on the matching shapes.

Ladybug Puzzle Game

Cut large ladybug shapes out of red posterboard, one for every two children. Cut each shape in half to make two puzzle pieces. Attach the same number of black self-stick circles to each half of a puzzle; for example, attach two dots on both halves of one puzzle, three dots on both halves of another puzzle, etc. Mix up all of the pieces and give one to each of your children. Then have the children move around the room and try to find their "puzzle partners" by matching up their puzzle pieces. When all of the ladybug puzzles have been put together, mix up the pieces and play the game again.

Ladybug Number Books

For each of your children, cut five large ladybug shapes out of red construction paper. Stack the shapes together, punch two holes on the left-hand side, and tie with yarn to make a book. Use a black felt tip marker to number the pages from 1 to 5. Give a book and 15 black self-stick circles to each child. Help the children put the appropriate number of circles on their pages according to the number written on each one.

Gone Fishing

Cut various sizes of fish shapes out of construction paper. Cover them with clear self-stick paper, if desired. Place the fish shapes in a dishpan "lake" and a find a stick a little longer than half of the fish shapes. Let your children take turns reaching into the lake and pulling out a fish shape. If the fish is smaller than the measuring stick, have the child put it back in the lake. If the fish is longer than the stick, have the child say, "It's a keeper," and put it in a fishing net.

Extension: Have the children arrange the fish according to size or sort them according to color.

Five Little Fish

Cut five simple fish shapes out of felt and place them on a flannelboard. Let your children take turns removing the fish as indicated, as you recite the poem that follows.

Five little fish swimming by the shore.

One got caught, and then there were four.

Four little fish swimming in the sea.

One got caught, and then there were three.

Three little fish in the ocean blue.

One got caught, and then there were two.

Two little fish swimming in the sun.

One got caught, and then there was one.

One little fish, swimming for home,

Decided it was best never to roam.

Jean Warren

Funny Frogs

Cut five frog shapes, such as those shown in the illustration, out of green felt and place them on a flannelboard. Then recite the poem below, letting your children take turns removing one frog at the end of each verse.

Five funny frogs fretting on the floor.
One jumped away, and that left four.
Four funny frogs fooling in a tree.
One jumped down, and that left three.
Three funny frogs—just a funny few.
One flipped out, and that left two.
Two funny frogs having froggy fun.
One hopped away, and that left one.
One funny frog, thinking he's a hero,
Left to tell his tale, and that left zero.

Susan M. Paprocki

Totline® Books

For parents, teachers, and others who work with young children

TEACHING THEMES

THEME-A-SAURUS®

Classroom-tested, around-the-curriculum activities organized into imaginative units. Great for implementing a child-directed program.

Theme-A-Saurus

Theme-A-Saurus II

Toddler Theme-A-Saurus

Alphabet Theme-A-Saurus

Nursery Rhyme Theme-A-Saurus

Storytime Theme-A-Saurus

BUSY BEES SERIES

Designed for two's and three's—these seasonal books help young children discover the world through their senses. Activity and learning ideas include simple songs, rhymes, snack ideas, movement activities, and art and science projects.

Busy Bees—SPRING

Busy Bees—SUMMER

Busy Bees—FALL

Busy Bees—WINTER

PLAY & LEARN SERIES

This creative, hands-on series explores the versatile play-and-learn opportunities of familiar objects.

Play & Learn with Stickers

Play & Learn with Paper Shapes and Borders

Play & Learn with Magnets

Play & Learn with Rubber Stamps

Play & Learn with Photos

GREAT BIG THEMES

Giant units that explore a specific theme through art, language, learning games, science, movement activities, music, and snack ideas. Includes reproducible theme alphabet cards and patterns.

Space

Farm

Zoo

Circus

CELEBRATIONS SERIES

Easy, practical ideas for celebrating holidays and special days around the world. Plus ideas for making ordinary days special.

Small World Celebrations

Special Day Celebrations

Great Big Holiday Celebrations

EXPLORING SERIES

Encourage exploration with hands-on activities that emphasize all the curriculum areas.

Exploring Sand and the Desert

Exploring Water and the Ocean

Exploring Wood and the Forest

NUTRITION

SNACKS SERIES

This series provides easy and educational recipes for healthful, delicious eating and additional opportunities for learning.

Super Snacks

Healthy Snacks

Teaching Snacks

Multicultural Snacks

LANGUAGE

CUT & TELL CUTOUTS

Each cutout folder includes a delightful tale, color figures for turning into manipulatives, and reproducible activity pages.

COLOR RHYMES *Rhymes and activities to teach color concepts.*

Cobbler, Cobbler

Hickety, Pickety

Mary, Mary, Quite Contrary

The Mulberry Bush

The Muffin Man

The Three Little Kittens

NUMBER RHYMES *Emphasize numbers and counting.*

Hickory, Dickory Dock

Humpty Dumpty

1, 2, Buckle My Shoe

Old Mother Hubbard

Rabbit, Rabbit, Carrot Eater

Twinkle, Twinkle, Little Star

NURSERY TALES *Enhance language development with these classic favorites.*

The Gingerbread Kid

Henny Penny

The Three Bears

The Three Billy Goats Gruff

Little Red Riding Hood

The Three Little Pigs

The Big, Big Carrot

The Country Mouse and the City Mouse

The Elves & the Shoemaker

The Hare and the Tortoise

The Little Red Hen

Stone Soup

TAKE-HOME RHYME BOOKS SERIES

Make prereading books for young children with these reproducible stories. Great confidence builders!

Alphabet & Number Rhymes

Color, Shape & Season Rhymes

Object Rhymes

Animal Rhymes

MUSIC

PIGGYBACK® SONGS

New songs sung to the tunes of childhood favorites. No music to read! Easy for adults and children to learn. Chorded for guitar or autoharp.

Piggyback Songs

More Piggyback Songs

Piggyback Songs for Infants & Toddlers

Piggyback Songs in Praise of God

Piggyback Songs in Praise of Jesus

Holiday Piggyback Songs

Animal Piggyback Songs

Piggyback Songs for School

Piggyback Songs to Sign

Spanish Piggyback Songs

More Piggyback Songs for School

Totline Books are available at local parent and teacher stores

TEACHING RESOURCES

BEAR HUGS® SERIES

Think you can't make it through another day? Give yourself a Bear Hug! This unique series focuses on positive behavior in young children and how to encourage it on a group and individual level.

Meals and Snacks

Cleanup

Nap Time

Remembering the Rules

Staying in Line

Circle Time

Transition Times

Time Out

Saying Goodbye

Saving the Earth

Getting Along

Fostering Self-Esteem

Being Afraid

Being Responsible

Being Healthy

Welcoming Children

Accepting Change

Respecting Others

1001 SERIES

These super reference books are filled with just the right tip, prop, or poem for your projects.

1001 Teaching Props

1001 Teaching Tips

1001 Rhymes & Fingerplays

THE BEST OF TOTLINE®

A collection of the best ideas from more than a decade's worth of Totline Newsletters. Month-by-month resource guides include instant, hands-on ideas for around-the-curriculum activities. 400 pages

LEARNING & CARING ABOUT SERIES

Developmentally appropriate activities to help children explore, understand, and appreciate the world around them. Includes reproducible parent flyers.

Our World

Our Selves

Our Town

MIX AND MATCH PATTERNS

Simple patterns, each printed in four sizes.

Animal Patterns

Everyday Patterns

Nature Patterns

Holiday Patterns

1•2•3 SERIES

Open-ended, age-appropriate, cooperative, and no-lose experiences for working with preschool children.

1•2•3 Art

1•2•3 Games

1•2•3 Colors

1•2•3 Puppets

1•2•3 Reading & Writing

1•2•3 Rhymes, Stories & Songs

1•2•3 Math

1•2•3 Science

1•2•3 Shapes

101 TIPS FOR DIRECTORS

Great ideas for managing a preschool or daycare! These hassle-free, handy hints help directors juggle the many hats they wear.

Staff and Parent Self-Esteem

Parent Communication

Health and Safety

Marketing Your Center

Resources for You and Your Center

Child Development Training

FOUR SEASONS SERIES

Each book in this delightful series provides fun, hands-on activity ideas for each season of the year.

Four Seasons–Movement

Four Seasons–Science

PARENTING RESOURCES

A YEAR OF FUN

These age-specific books provide information about how young children are growing and changing and what parents can do to lay a strong foundation for later learning. Calendarlike pages, designed to be displayed, offer developmentally appropriate activity suggestions for each month—plus practical parenting advice!

Just for Babies

Just for One's

Just for Two's

Just for Three's

Just for Four's

Just for Five's

TEACHING HOUSE SERIES

This new series helps parents become aware of the everyday opportunities for teaching their children. The tools for learning are all around the house and everywhere you go. Easy-to-follow directions for using ordinary materials combine family fun with learning.

Teaching House

Teaching Town

Teaching Trips

CHILDREN'S STORIES

Totline's children's stories are called Teaching Tales because they are two books in one—a storybook and an activity book with fun ideas to expand upon the themes of the story. Perfect for a variety of ages. Each book is written by Jean Warren.

Kids Celebrate the Alphabet

Ellie the Evergreen

The Wishing Fish

The Bear and the Mountain

HUFF AND PUFF® AROUND THE YEAR SERIES

Huff and Puff are two endearing, childlike clouds that will take your children on a new learning adventure each month.

Huff and Puff's Snowy Day

Huff and Puff on Groundhog Day

Huff and Puff's Hat Relay

Huff and Puff's April Showers

Huff and Puff's Hawaiian Rainbow

Huff and Puff Go to Camp

Huff and Puff on Fourth of July

Huff and Puff Around the World

Huff and Puff Go to School

Huff and Puff on Halloween

Huff and Puff on Thanksgiving

Huff and Puff's Foggy Christmas

Totline Books are available at local parent and teacher stores

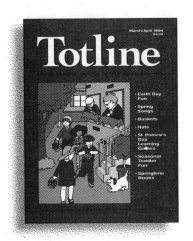
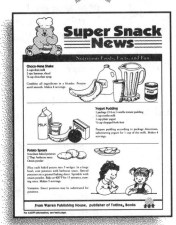